Moving to the

UNITED STATES

By Katacha Díaz

Scott Foresman
is an imprint of

Glenview, Illinois • Boston, Massachusetts • Chandler, Arizona •
Upper Saddle River, New Jersey

Photographs

Every effort has been made to secure permission and provide appropriate credit for photographic material. The publisher deeply regrets any omission and pledges to correct errors called to its attention in subsequent editions.

Unless otherwise acknowledged, photographs are the property of Pearson Education, Inc.
Most photos courtesy of Katacha Diaz. All rights reserved.

Photo locators denoted as follows: Top (T), Center (C), Bottom (B), Left (L), Right (R), Background (Bkgd)

Opener: (L) ©Katacha Diaz, (R) Steve Gorton and Karl Shone/©DK Images; **1** ©Katacha Diaz; **3** ©Katacha Diaz; **4** (Bkgd) ©Cartesia/Getty Images, (Inset) ©Katacha Diaz; **5** (L) ©Katacha Diaz, (L) ©Michael Moran/©DK Images, (R) ©Steve Gorton and Karl Shone/©DK Images; **6** (Inset) ©Design Pics/Jupiter Images, (Bkgd) ©Michael Moran/©DK Images; **7** ©Katacha Diaz; **8** (TL, B) ©Katacha Diaz; **10** ©Katacha Diaz; **11** (R, L) ©Katacha Diaz; **12** ©Katacha Diaz.

ISBN 13: 978-0-328-47257-4
ISBN 10:   0-328-47257-3

7 8 9 10 V010 16 15 14 13

Table of Contents

Katacha as a Child

My name is Katacha Díaz. I was born in Washington, D.C. When I was nine months old, my parents and I returned to Peru. That is where my father was born.

As a girl, I dreamed of being a writer. I loved to tell stories. I wrote my first story in a letter to my grandparents.

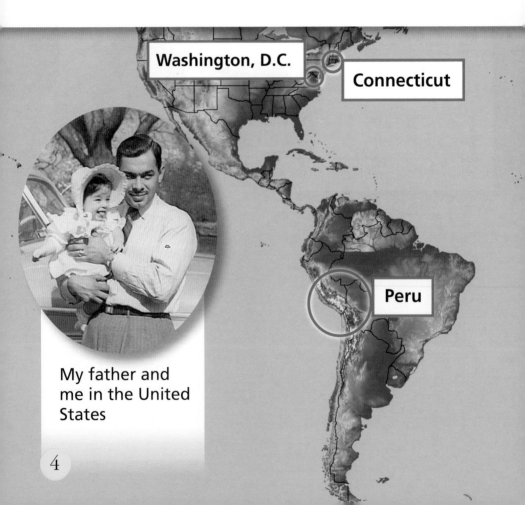

Washington, D.C.

Connecticut

Peru

My father and me in the United States

Immigrating to the United States

In 1960 my family immigrated to the United States. I was fifteen years old. We moved so that my sisters and I could go to good schools.

It wasn't easy moving from our home in Peru. We left behind my grandmother, uncles, aunts, and cousins.

We traveled across the United States and settled in Greenwich, Connecticut. The first snow I ever saw was a big blizzard. It covered our family's car!

Me at age 15, in passport photo

Life in Connecticut

Life in Greenwich was hard. Some people wanted us to go back to Peru. They didn't like our accent. They didn't like how we looked.

Then I discovered the public library. I began to read a lot. Reading made me feel better.

In our home, we spoke two languages—Spanish and English. At school, my sisters and I spoke English with an accent. Some kids made fun of the way we sounded and the things we said. I felt a lot of peer pressure to lose my accent.

My mother, my sisters, and me in Connecticut

I missed my friends and family in Peru.
I missed the Sunday tamales lunch at my
grandparent's house there.

In Greenwich, my mother tried to make us feel better. She made us tamale pie. She fixed our favorite dessert, called flan. My father played Spanish music, and we danced the *merengue*. For a little while, we felt as if we were back home in Peru.

Sunday lunch at my grandparent's house

Never Give Up

I was homesick and lonely. I filled the hours by reading library books and writing letters. I also got good grades at school because it was important to my family.

It took a long time for me to feel as if I belonged in my new country. Sometimes I felt very alone. But the United States gave me the chance to follow my dreams.

My college graduation

I know that I'm a stronger person because of the hard times I faced.